Dez Bryant

By Jon M. Fishman

AMAZING
ATHLETES

Lerner Publications ◆ Minneapolis

Lerner Publications Company
A division of Lerner Publishing Group, Inc.
241 First Avenue North
Minneapolis, MN 55401 USA

For reading levels and more information, look up this title at www.lernerbooks.com.

Library of Congress Cataloging-in-Publication Data

Fishman, Jon M.
    Dez Bryant / by Jon M. Fishman.
        pages cm. — (Amazing athletes)
    Includes index.
        ISBN 978-1-4677-7919-7 (lb : alk. paper) — ISBN 978-1-4677-8110-7 (pb : alk. paper) —
    ISBN 978-1-4677-8543-3 (eb pdf)
        1. Bryant, Dez. 2. Football players—United States—Biography—Juvenile literature. I. Title.
GV939.B788F57 2016
796.332092—dc23 [B]   2015002524

Manufactured in the United States of America
1 – BP – 7/15/15

TABLE OF CONTENTS

Dez Bryant scores a touchdown on a 65-yard catch during a game against the Washington Redskins.

RECORD SETTER

Dallas Cowboys **wide receiver** Dez Bryant leaned forward and let his arms hang loosely at his sides. "Hut, hut!" **Quarterback** Tony Romo took the snap. He quickly turned to his left and flung the ball to Dez. The young receiver faked to his left and then cut quickly to the right. Dez was in the clear! He streaked down the sideline for a 65-yard touchdown.

Tony Romo of the Dallas Cowboys throws a touchdown pass to Dez Bryant.

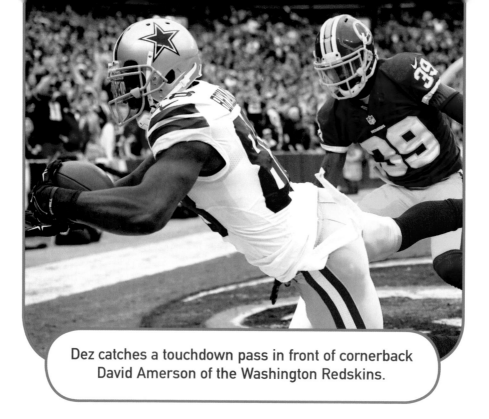

Dez catches a touchdown pass in front of cornerback David Amerson of the Washington Redskins.

Dez and the Cowboys were playing against the Washington Redskins on December 28, 2014. Dez's first-quarter score put the Cowboys ahead, 10–7. Dallas had already secured a place in the **playoffs** and a chance to play in the Super Bowl. But Cowboys fans were fired up for the game anyway. Washington is one of Dallas's oldest **rivals**.

Fans were also excited to see if Dez could

set a new team record for most receiving touchdowns in a season. The Cowboys have been a team since 1960. In all those years, no Dallas player had caught more than 15 touchdown passes in a single season. After Dez's long touchdown in the first quarter, he needed only one more to set the record.

It didn't take long for Dez to score his 16th touchdown. The Cowboys got the ball back and raced down the field. This time, Romo threw a deep pass to Dez in the **end zone**. Dez snatched the ball out of the air and tapped both his feet on the ground before going out of bounds. Touchdown!

The Cowboys have won the Super Bowl five times. This is the second most of any team. Only the Pittsburgh Steelers have won more Super Bowls.

Dez's touchdowns were just the beginning of a successful game for the Cowboys. Dallas crushed Washington, 44–17. After the game, Dez was focused on the upcoming playoffs.

Dez catches his second touchdown pass of the game as Amerson tries to stop him.

"We've worked too hard and have got an opportunity to do something special," he said. But Dez had already done something special by setting a new touchdown record. "Oh man, it feels good," he said.

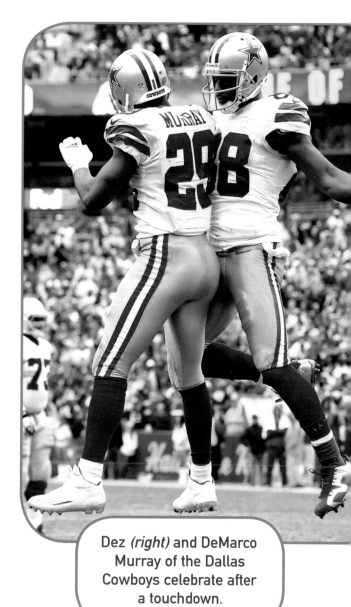

Dez *(right)* and DeMarco Murray of the Dallas Cowboys celebrate after a touchdown.

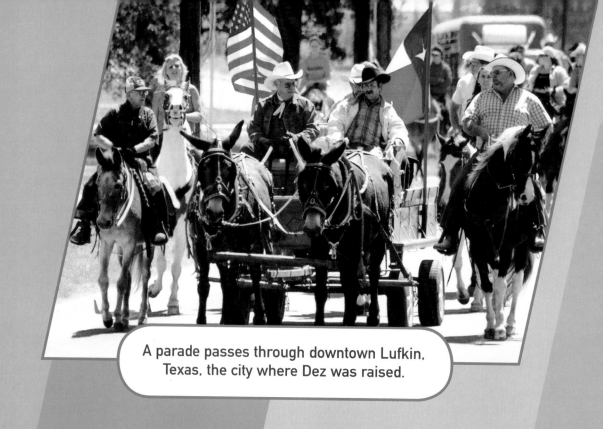

A parade passes through downtown Lufkin, Texas, the city where Dez was raised.

GETTING BY

On November 4, 1988, Desmond Demond Bryant was born in Galveston County, Texas. His family called him Dez. The Bryants soon moved to nearby Lufkin, Texas.

Angela Bryant had been just 14 years old when she gave birth to Dez. By the time Angela was 18 years old, she had three children. Dez's father was in and out of his son's life.

Life in Lufkin was difficult for the Bryant family. Angela did her best to provide for her children. She worked as a cook and earned less than five dollars an hour. She didn't have enough money to buy her children food, clothes, and other things they needed. "I was broke, broke," Angela said. "I was as broke as you can be broke."

Dez sits next to his mother, Angela Bryant, in Dallas in 2012.

Angela began selling illegal drugs to earn more money. She also began using drugs. In 1997, Angela was arrested and spent 18 months in jail. Eight-year-old Dez stayed with his father. The time Angela spent in jail away from her family convinced her to give up drugs for good.

Dez moved back in with his father for a short time around eighth or ninth grade.

When Dez was 10 years old, he moved back in with his mother. He was ready to play organized football for the first time. Angela signed him up for a youth league.

Dez fell in love with football. He liked the sport so much that he didn't want to go on a trip to a Six Flags amusement park that would have forced him to miss a game. "Momma, I can't go [to Six Flags]," Dez said. "If I go, we're

Dez gave up a day of roller coasters and other rides at Six Flags amusement park to help his youth football team score a victory.

not going to win." Dez skipped the trip and played in the football game instead. He scored a touchdown, and his team won, 6–0.

A young Dez poses for a picture in high school.

DOING WHAT IT TAKES

In 2003, Dez started as a freshman at Lufkin High
School (LHS). He joined his school's football and
track and field teams. Dez was tall, lean, and
athletic. He let his natural gifts carry him. He
didn't have to try very hard to score touchdowns
or win races.

But Dez also didn't try very hard in the

classroom. He worked just hard enough to pass his classes. "I wasn't a dummy," Dez said. "When I felt like doing [the work], I did—and it was no problem."

After Dez's sophomore year at LHS, he changed his attitude about school and football. He decided that he wanted to play in the National Football League (NFL) one day. To reach that goal, he would have to work harder on the football field.

Dez catches a pass during his time at LHS.

He would also have to spend more time on his schoolwork to qualify for college. In college, athletes train and compete against other top players. It is an important step for athletes who want to play in the NFL.

In 2005, Dez's junior season in high school, his new focus on the football field paid off. He caught 48 passes that year, the most on his LHS **varsity** team. In 2006, Dez led his team again by catching 53 passes. He also scored an incredible 21 touchdowns that year.

After his senior season, Rivals.com ranked Dez as the ninth-best high school wide receiver in the United States.

Scouts around the country believed Dez could be a star player in college. But to be accepted by a college with a big-time football team, Dez would have to improve his grades.

Dez impressed scouts with his work on the field.

He would also have to earn an acceptable score on the American College Testing (ACT) exam.

Dez put more effort into his schoolwork and brought his grades up. And with the help of people at LHS, such as math teacher Jody Anderson, he got a good score on the ACT. "I've taught school for thirty-five years, and I've never been prouder of a student than I am of [Dez]," said Anderson. "I admired what he was trying to do and how hard he worked to do it."

Oklahoma State's Boone Pickens Stadium

COWBOYS STAR

Colleges all around the country were eager to add Dez to their football teams. He received interest from some of the most successful schools in the nation. He decided to take a **scholarship** that was offered by the Oklahoma State University (OSU) Cowboys.

Dez began school at OSU in 2007. Many first-year college football players need a year of practice and training before they are ready to play. But Dez proved that he was up for the challenge of playing right away. The 18-year-old freshman immediately showed great promise. In a game against the University of Kansas, Dez reeled in 155 receiving yards. This was the most receiving yards in a game for an OSU freshman in the team's history.

Dez makes a catch during an Oklahoma State Cowboys game.

In 12 games, Dez caught 43 passes and scored six touchdowns. Both were the second-best marks on the team.

As a sophomore in 2008, Dez was one of the best college players in the country. He scored 19 touchdowns in 12 games. Only one player in the country caught more touchdown passes. Dez snagged 87 passes for almost 1,500 yards.

Dez catches a pass and runs in for a touchdown during the first quarter of the 2008 Holiday Bowl.

Dez scores a touchdown at the Holiday Bowl.

The Cowboys won nine games in 2008 and played in the Holiday Bowl. Dez was slowed by a knee injury during the Holiday Bowl. But the sore knee didn't stop him from scoring a touchdown. He also tallied 13 catches for 168 yards. It was the most receiving yards in Holiday Bowl history. Despite Dez's successful plays, the Cowboys lost the game to the University of Oregon, 42–31.

Excitement was high for Dez and OSU in 2009. Some fans and reporters believed Dez could win the **Heisman Trophy**. But Dez's season ended after just three games because he broke a rule off the field. Dez had spent time with former NFL player Deion Sanders. The two had trained together, and Sanders bought Dez lunch. The **National Collegiate Athletic Association (NCAA)** has strict rules about how athletes spend their time. College players are not allowed to receive money or gifts, such as free lunches, from former players. When the NCAA asked Dez about his time with Sanders, Dez lied. When the NCAA found out he lied, Dez was not allowed to play for the rest of the season.

Deion Sanders played for the Dallas Cowboys from 1995 to 1999. He also played several seasons of Major League Baseball for various teams.

After a successful time playing for OSU, Dez began his journey to play in the NFL.

AMERICA'S RECEIVER

Dez could have returned to OSU for the 2010 season. But most fans and scouts thought he was ready for the NFL. Dez decided it was time to move on from college ball. He entered the 2010 NFL **draft**.

On the day of the draft, Dez's friends and family gathered in Dez's home. There were also television cameras there to film their reaction. When the Dallas Cowboys chose Dez with the 24th pick in the draft, everyone in Dez's home cheered. Dez dropped to his knees with tears in his eyes as his mother hugged him. A few

Dez hugs his mother after being selected by the Dallas Cowboys in the first round of the 2010 NFL draft.

weeks later, he signed a contract with the Cowboys worth almost $12 million!

As a **rookie** in 2010, Dez scored six touchdowns. In 2011, he racked up nine touchdowns. Dez has improved his touchdown total every year that he's been in the NFL.

Dez scores a touchdown as Chris Houston of the Detroit Lions defends him.

The 2014 season was Dez's best yet. His team saw great success that season too, winning 12 games and the top spot in their **division**.

They beat the Detroit Lions in the first round of the playoffs, 24–20. Their next playoff opponent was the Green Bay Packers.

The Packers held Dez in check for most of the game. With Green Bay ahead by five points in the fourth quarter, the Cowboys faced fourth down and two yards to go. With the game on the line, the team turned to their star player. They would use Dez to try to make a big play. Green Bay thought Dallas would run the ball and left only one man outside to cover Dez.

Fans have long referred to the Dallas Cowboys by the nickname America's Team.

But Romo threw the ball deep to Dez. The tall receiver leaped and snared the ball in his big hands. He stretched for the **goal line** as he fell to the ground. But when Dez hit the ground, the ball popped out of his hands. No catch! Green Bay won the game, 26–21.

Although they lost the Green Bay game, the media talked about Dez's play again and again, creating a buzz. And his fans and teammates were thrilled that Dez had set the Cowboys' record for touchdown catches that season. But Dez has his eyes on a bigger prize—the Super Bowl.

Dez makes a catch along the sidelines as Green Bay Packers player Sam Shields tries to stop him.

Dez signs autographs for excited fans.

"[The record] is cool, but there's nothing to be excited about," he said. "We know what we're after." Many fans, reporters, and fellow players believe Dez has the talent to bring a Super Bowl victory to Dallas.

Selected Career Highlights

2014 Caught 88 passes and 16 touchdowns for the
Dallas Cowboys
Voted to the NFL Pro Bowl for the second time

2013 Caught 93 passes and 13 touchdowns for the
Dallas Cowboys
Voted to the NFL Pro Bowl for the first time

2012 Caught 92 passes and 12 touchdowns for the
Dallas Cowboys

2011 Caught 63 passes and nine touchdowns for the
Dallas Cowboys

2010 Chosen by the Dallas Cowboys with the 24th
pick in the first round of the NFL draft
Caught 45 passes and six touchdowns for the
Dallas Cowboys

2009 Played three games for Oklahoma State University
before being suspended

2008 Set the Oklahoma State University record with 19
touchdown catches
Set the Holiday Bowl record with 168 yards receiving

2007 Played 12 games as a freshman for Oklahoma State University
Finished second on his team with six touchdown catches

2006 Caught 53 passes for 1,207 yards and 21 touchdowns for Lufkin
High School

2005 Caught 48 passes for 1,025 yards and 16 touchdowns for Lufkin
High School

Glossary

division: a group of teams that play against one another. Division winners move on to the playoffs.

draft: a yearly event in which teams take turns choosing new players from a group

end zone: the area beyond the goal line at each end of a football field. A team scores a touchdown when they reach the other team's end zone.

goal line: a line that appears at both ends of a football field. The ball must break the plane of the goal line to score a touchdown.

Heisman Trophy: an award given each year to college football's most outstanding player

National Collegiate Athletic Association (NCAA): a group that organizes and oversees college athletics in the United States

playoffs: a series of games held to determine a champion

quarterback: a player whose main job is to throw passes

rivals: teams that compete against one another for the same prize

rookie: a first-year player

scholarship: money awarded to students to help pay for college

scouts: football experts who watch players closely to judge their abilities

varsity: the top team at a school

wide receiver: a player whose main job is to catch passes

Further Reading & Websites

Bowker, Paul. *Playing Pro Football*. Minneapolis: Lerner Publications, 2015.

Kennedy, Mike, and Mark Stewart. *Touchdown: The Power and Precision of Football's Perfect Play*. Minneapolis: Millbrook Press, 2010.

Savage, Jeff. *Tony Romo*. Minneapolis: Lerner Publications, 2011.

Dallas Cowboys Website
http://www.dallascowboys.com
The official website of the Cowboys includes team schedules, news, profiles of past and present players and coaches, and much more.

NFL Website
http://www.nfl.com
The NFL's official website provides fans with recent news stories, statistics, biographies of players and coaches, and information about games.

Sports Illustrated Kids
http://www.sikids.com
The *Sports Illustrated Kids* website includes blogs, photos, and videos about many sports, including football.

Index

Photo Acknowledgments

The images in this book are used with the permission of: AP Photo/James D Smith, p. 4; © Patrick Smith/Getty Images, pp. 5, 6, 9 © Mitchell Layton/Getty Images, p. 8; AP Photo/The Lufkin Daily News/Joel Andrews, p. 10; AP Photo/ Nomaan Merchant, p. 11; © Tony Gutierrez/AP/CORBIS, p. 13; Courtesy of Todd Quick/Lufkin High School, pp. 14, 15; Andrew Fielding/SCG/ ZUMAPRESS.com/Newscom, p. 17; AP Photo/Icon Sportswire, p. 18; © Scott Cunningham/Getty Images, p. 19; Louis Lopez/Cal Sport Media/Newscom, pp. 20, 21; Alan Smith/Cal Sport Media/Newscom, p. 23; AP Photo/Tom Pennington, p. 24; AP Photo/LM Otero, p. 25; AP Photo/G. Newman Lowrance, p. 27; AP Photo/Darren Abate, p. 28; AP Photo/Sharon Ellman, p. 29.

Front cover: Steven Bisig/USA Today Sports/Newscom.

Main body text set in Caecilia LT Std 55 Roman 16/28.
Typeface provided by Adobe Systems.